THE INDUS VALLEY

BY MADELINE TYLER

KidHaven
PUBLISHING

UNLOCKING ANCIENT CIVILIZATIONS

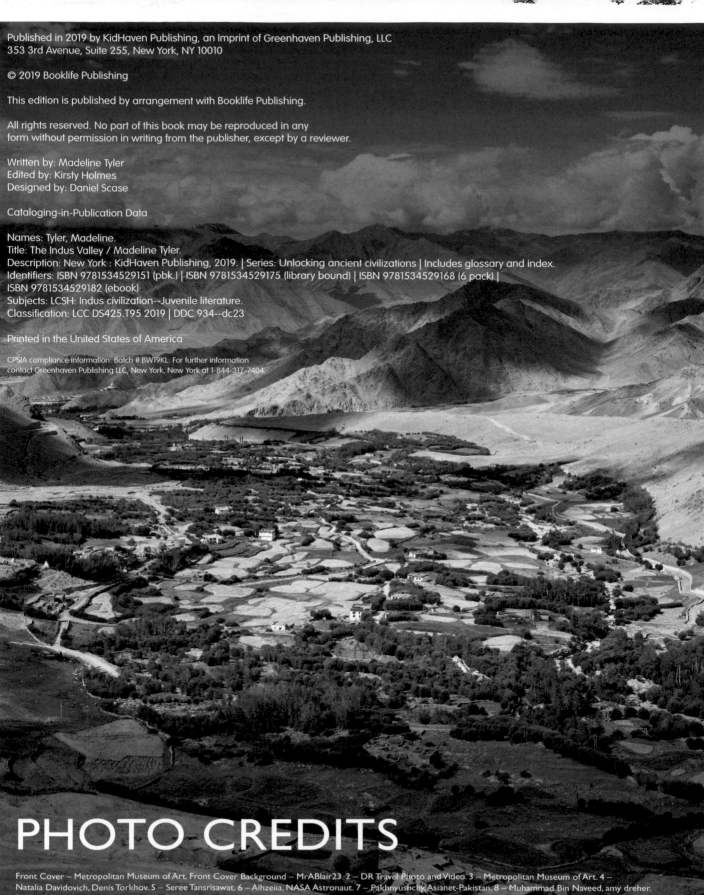

Published in 2019 by KidHaven Publishing, an Imprint of Greenhaven Publishing, LLC
353 3rd Avenue, Suite 255, New York, NY 10010

© 2019 Booklife Publishing

This edition is published by arrangement with Booklife Publishing.

Written by: Madeline Tyler
Edited by: Kirsty Holmes
Designed by: Daniel Scase

Cataloging-in-Publication Data

Names: Tyler, Madeline.
Title: The Indus Valley / Madeline Tyler.
Description: New York : KidHaven Publishing, 2019. | Series: Unlocking ancient civilizations | Includes glossary and index.
Identifiers: ISBN 9781534529151 (pbk.) | ISBN 9781534529175 (library bound) | ISBN 9781534529168 (6 pack) |
ISBN 9781534529182 (ebook)
Subjects: LCSH: Indus civilization--Juvenile literature.
Classification: LCC DS425.T95 2019 | DDC 934--dc23

Printed in the United States of America

CPSIA compliance information: Batch # BW19KL: For further information
contact Greenhaven Publishing LLC, New York, New York at 1-844-317-7404.

PHOTO CREDITS

Front Cover – Metropolitan Museum of Art. Front Cover Background – MrABlair23. 2 – DR Travel Photo and Video. 3 – Metropolitan Museum of Art. 4 –
Natalia Davidovich, Denis Torkhov. 5 – Seree Tansrisawat. 6 – Alhzeiia, NASA Astronaut. 7 – Pakhnyushchy, Asianet-Pakistan. 8 – Muhammad Bin Naveed, amy dreher.
9 – UNESCO, Saqib Qayyum. 10 – suronin, Saeed Husain Rizvi. 11 – Saeed Husain Rizvi. 12 – saiko3p, Bernard Gagnon. 13 – Olga Gorevan, Rama's Arrow. 14 –
Jen with modifications by Ismoon, Mohenjodaro archaeological site. 15 – Tukaram.Karve. 16 – Miya.m, Thomas Schoch, Wikicommons, Diliff. 17 – Biswarup Ganguly.
18 – Saurav022, Ozphotoguy. 19 – Royroydeb, PhotocechCZ. 20 – Wikicommons, Yann. 21 – Metropolitan Museum of Art, Mamoon Mengal. 22 – Royroydeb, Ismoon.
23 – Mukerjee, Hans Hillewaert. 24 – bodom, Asholove. 25 – Saeed Husain Rizvi, suronin. 26 – ARTiFACTS, Ville Miettinen. 27 – Jerry Horbert, paul prescott.
28 & 29 – BigIndianFootage, Saeed Husain Rizvi, DR Travel Photo and Video, Saqib Qayyum, Darkydoors, Asianet-Pakistan, Metropolitan Museum of Art.
By Saeed Husain Rizvi, Muhammad Bin Naveed, Usman.pg, Mamoon Mengal. 32 – Metropolitan Museum of Art. Images are courtesy of Shutterstock.com.
With thanks to Getty Images, Thinkstock Photo and iStockphoto.

THE INDUS VALLEY

CONTENTS

All words that appear like *this* are explained in the glossary on page 31.

THE INDUS VALLEY

THE Indus Valley is an area in modern-day India and Pakistan that was once home to one of the earliest and largest **civilizations** in the world. The Indus Valley Civilization developed along the Indus River in around 2600 **B.C.** and reached its peak one hundred years later, in around 2500 B.C., when it covered more than 386,100 square miles (1 millon km²) of land. By this point, historians believe that there were more than 2,000 **settlements** across the civilization. Some were small villages and others were large cities like Harappa and Mohenjo-daro.

PEOPLE OFTEN MADE KNIVES AND SPEARHEADS FROM BRONZE.

The Indus Valley was one the largest Bronze Age civilizations. The Bronze Age was a period in history when people stopped using stone and began using bronze, a mixture of tin and copper, to make tools and weapons. Some other Bronze Age civilizations include Mesopotamia in the Middle East, ancient Egypt, and the Shang Dynasty in China.

The Indus River is over 1,860 miles (3,000 km) long and is the longest river in Pakistan. The river begins in the Himalayan mountains in China and flows about 1,990 miles (3,200 km) through Pakistan and India towards the coast and into the Arabian Sea. The river provided the Indus people with drinking water, a place to wash, and water for their crops. The area around the river in the Indus Valley was very green and *fertile* and was perfect for farming.

THE INDUS VALLEY CIVILIZATION IS NAMED AFTER THE INDUS RIVER AND VALLEY WHERE THE FIRST SIGNS OF THE CIVILIZATION WERE DISCOVERED.

People began farming in the Indus Valley in around 4000 B.C. They were very successful farmers and used the crops to feed themselves and trade with other civilizations. The small farming villages grew and developed, and around 1,000 years later in 3000 B.C. the first cities were built.

TOWN PLANNING

TOWNS and cities in the Indus Valley were planned very carefully. In major cities like Mohenjo-daro and Harappa, the roads were very straight and were laid out in a ***grid system***. The roads ran from north to south and from east to west, and split the city into square or rectangular sections called blocks. The Indus people built the first planned cities in the world, but the method was soon being used in other civilizations. Many cities such as Barcelona in Spain and Beijing in China use the grid system today.

BARCELONA, SPAIN

Cities that are not planned are called organic or unplanned cities. Organic cities like Boston in Massachusetts grow slowly outward from the center. They begin as small villages before growing into towns and then cities. These cities are not organized in blocks and do not usually have straight roads.

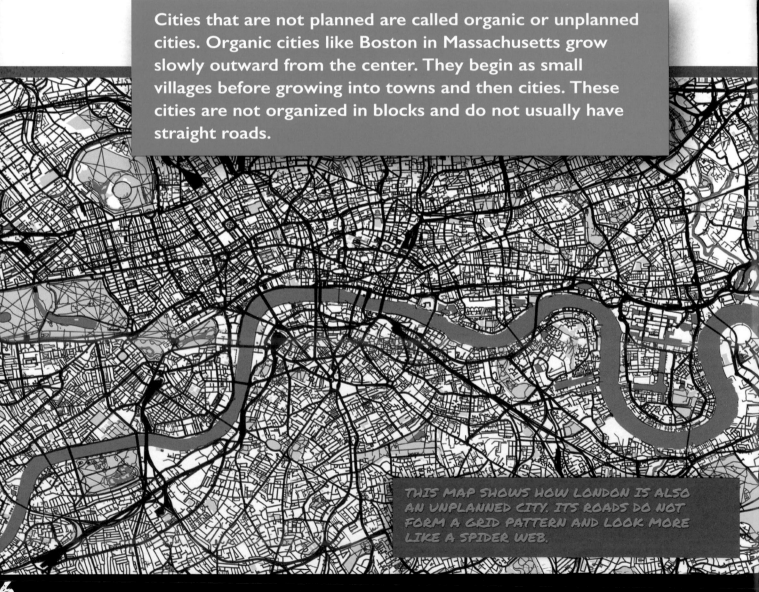

THIS MAP SHOWS HOW LONDON IS ALSO AN UNPLANNED CITY. ITS ROADS DO NOT FORM A GRID PATTERN AND LOOK MORE LIKE A SPIDER WEB.

Historians are not certain whether cities in the Indus Valley were independent city-states or part of a large empire. City-states are made up of the city and often its surrounding area. They have their own ruler and *government* and usually have a different culture and way of life than other city-states around them. An empire is a group of different nations and people that are ruled by one leader from a capital.

THE ANCIENT GREEK CITY OF ATHENS IS AN EXAMPLE OF A CITY-STATE IN ANTIQUITY.

No temples, palaces, or statues of Indus leaders have been found in any cities of the Indus Valley Civilization, so it is difficult to know very much about how their settlements and societies were organized. There may have been one king who ruled from a city such as Mohenjo-daro or Harappa, or many different leaders who each had control of a city or region.

SOME STRUCTURES, LIKE THE *CITADEL* IN MOHENJO-DARO, STILL EXIST AND HAVE TAUGHT HISTORIANS ABOUT CITIES IN THE INDUS VALLEY.

THE Indus Valley's two main cities, Harappa and Mohenjo-daro, are known as the "twin capitals" of the civilization. Harappa was the first city discovered in the Indus Valley. It is in present-day Pakistan and was first found in **A.D.** 1826. Groups of ***archaeologists*** began digging up the ruins in 1920 to study them and find out more about the people who lived there. Historians believe that people lived in Harappa between 3800 and 1500 B.C. and, at its largest, it was home to around 25,000 people. The city was surrounded by a wall and had a large citadel built on top of a mound of earth.

Harappa was towards the edge of the Indus Valley and therefore would probably have served as a gateway city into the center of the region. It would have been a very busy and important city with many people passing in and out.

SEVERAL ARTIFACTS, INCLUDING PIECES OF POTTERY, HAVE BEEN DISCOVERED IN HARAPPA.

MOHENJO-DARO

Mohenjo-daro was rediscovered in Pakistan in 1922. It was the largest city in the Indus Valley and had around 40,000 people living there at one point. Both Harappa and Mohenjo-daro were planned in a grid, with straight roads and blocks of buildings. The buildings were made from mud bricks and were often several **stories** high. The mud bricks were all a standard size and were baked at high temperatures in a **kiln**. The largest and most important buildings, including a citadel and the Great Bath, were built on top of a tall mound that overlooked the city. Religious ceremonies and rituals were held at the citadel, while historians think the Great Bath may have been used to wash people before attending these ceremonies.

THE GREAT BATH WAS SO BIG THAT IT WAS MORE LIKE A SWIMMING POOL THAN A BATH. IT WAS OVER 46 FEET (14 M) LONG AND OVER 6 FEET (2 M) DEEP.

Mohenjo-daro experienced many floods because of how closely it was built to the Indus River. These floods were so damaging that they may have even destroyed parts of the city and caused people to move away. Historians think that because of these floods, Harappa may have survived longer than Mohenjo-daro.

HOUSES IN THE INDUS VALLEY

LIKE other buildings, houses in the Indus Valley were made using mud bricks. They were several stories high and had flat roofs. The roof was used as an extra floor to dry crops and to sleep on in the summer when it was too warm to stay inside. The houses had doors that led out onto the street and stairs to reach the higher floors.

Poorer people had small homes that sometimes only had one room. Richer people had large houses made up of lots of rooms built around a courtyard. The courtyard was a large, open space with no roof that usually had a well to collect water from and plants growing in pots. There may have been a wooden balcony over the courtyard that people could walk over. Windows opened out to the courtyard but not onto the main street. This made sure no dirt or dust came into the house.

MOST HOUSES FROM THE INDUS VALLEY CIVILIZATION ARE NOW IN RUINS.

WELL

Houses in the Indus Valley usually had a bedroom with a simple wooden bed frame in it. The frames had strips of leather across them to lay on. Almost all houses also had a bathroom with a toilet and a shower tray. People stood over the shower tray and poured clean water from the well over themselves to keep clean. The dirty water washed away through a pipe into a drain in the street. The pipes of each home were all connected to the same drainage system that ran along the street.

ALL HOUSES WERE BUILT USING MUD BRICKS.

Richer people lived on the upper side of the city, close to the citadel, while poorer Indus people lived in houses that all looked similar to each other in the lower side of the city. Poor people were usually farmers or craftsmen and, although some of them did live in the cities, most *peasants* lived further out in the countryside.

PLUMBING AND DRAINAGE

MANDIR IN KOLKATA, INDIA

WELLS AND BATHS

NDUS cities had a well in the center where people could collect fresh, clean water. Some houses even had their own private wells. Wells meant that cool water could be brought up from underground and used for washing and drinking. Some of these wells were up to 66 feet (20 m) deep into the ground. Keeping clean was very important to the Indus people and historians believe that they bathed every day.

WELL

Cleanliness is also important in Hinduism, one of the main religions in present-day India. Before visiting a mandir (a Hindu temple), Hindus wash their feet and rinse their mouth out with water. They also bathe every morning as part of a daily ritual before worshipping at the family shrine. Historians have suggested that some Hindu beliefs may have come from Indus ideas about cleanliness and *purity*.

TOILETS

The Indus people were some of the first people in the world to have toilets. The toilets could be found in many Indus houses and were quite different from modern toilets. They had brick seats and did not flush. Instead, people had to pour jugs of water into them to clear them out. Any waste was carried in clay pipes into street drains under the ground and along the side of the road, and then into soak pits. It was then someone's job to dig out the soak pits and take the waste away. This kept the city and the area clean and stopped it from smelling bad.

In the ancient city of Dholavira, historians have found many large **reservoirs** made from mud bricks. The **climate** in the Indus Valley was very dry and the area did not receive much rain. Reservoirs collected rainwater that could be stored for a long time and used during a **drought**.

DHOLAVIRA

SOME OF THE EARLIEST RESERVOIRS AND WATER CHANNELS CAN BE FOUND IN THE ANCIENT CITY OF DHOLAVIRA.

EVERYDAY LIFE

RELIGION

HISTORIANS believe the Indus Valley was a peaceful civilization. Not many weapons have been found and they did not have an army. They spent a lot of time with their families working, playing, and dancing. Scribes taught children to read and write and priests taught them about the religion.

Historians have learned about religion in the Indus Valley by studying the images carved into *seals*. Some seals appear to show images of gods, while others are of animals that historians believe the Indus people worshipped and thought were *sacred*.

SEALS

STATUES LIKE THE DANCING GIRL SUGGEST THAT PEOPLE IN THE INDUS VALLEY ENJOYED DANCING. HISTORIANS ARE NOT SURE WHETHER THEY DANCED TO HONOR THE GODS OR JUST FOR FUN.

Some graves have been found in the Indus Valley where Indus people were buried with pots and small figures made from clay. Some people think this means that the Indus people believed in an afterlife where they could take these objects with them after they died.

MONEY

Unlike modern societies, people in the Indus Valley did not use money. Instead, they traded and exchanged different goods, like animals or sacks of grain, between each other and with other civilizations. Being rich in the Indus Valley did not mean you had a lot of money. Rich Indus people had a lot of land, lots of **cattle**, and plenty of crops and grain.

BULLOCK CARTS ARE STILL USED ALL AROUND INDIA TODAY.

TRADE

Trade is when you give someone a product or a service in exchange for something else. For example, someone may give someone else five bags of grain in payment for building their house. This is a trade. Merchants in the Indus Valley transported their goods to other cities in bullock carts.

Bullock carts were pulled by animals called oxen and had large, wooden wheels. Other merchants traveled very long distances to trade with people from Sumer, a city in Mesopotamia. They sailed with their goods on large ships across the Arabian Sea to Mesopotamia in the Middle East.

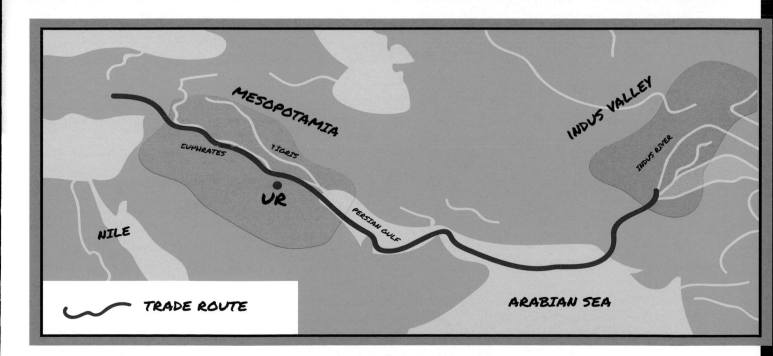

MESOPOTAMIA

EUPHRATES

TIGRIS

INDUS VALLEY

INDUS RIVER

UR

NILE

PERSIAN GULF

TRADE ROUTE

ARABIAN SEA

LIFE AS A CHILD

Not much is known about growing up in the Indus Valley, but historians believe that the children loved to play with toys and games. They played in the courtyards of their homes and on the flat roofs with their friends. Some common toys included miniature models of animals, such as cows and monkeys, made from clay. Some of the models had wheels and were attached to string so that they could be pulled along the ground. They also played board games with dice and counters. The dice had six sides with spots on them and were similar to modern dice that are used today. These may be some of the oldest dice in the world.

Historians believe that families in the Indus Valley may have kept animals such as monkeys, birds, snakes, or dogs as pets. The children might have cared for the animals and played with them, too.

RICH AND POOR

Life was different for people in the Indus Valley depending on whether they were **wealthy** or not. Peasants and craftspeople lived in small houses and wore simple dresses and **loincloths**. They worked very hard and children often had to help their parents with farming and hunting. Richer people wore tunics, more **expensive** dresses, and both men and women wore jewelry. The women also wore beads and headdresses in their hair.

PEOPLE THINK EVERYDAY LIFE IN THE INDUS VALLEY WOULD HAVE LOOKED SIMILAR TO THIS RECONSTRUCTION.

MARKETPLACES WERE COMMON IN THE INDUS VALLEY.

Some Indus people got very rich by working as traders and merchants. They exchanged very expensive goods such as rugs and jewels with people in other lands. The very richest people had servants and even possibly slaves working In their houses for them. Rich and poor people in the Indus Valley had to pay **taxes** to the government. These taxes were paid in crops that were stored in a large building called a granary, and could be shared with everyone during **famines** when there was a shortage of food.

FARMING

MOST people lived and worked in the countryside as farmers, making use of the fertile land. They grew lots of crops including wheat, barley, peas, mustard, and lentils as well as fruits such as grapes and melons that were used to feed the civilization. They prepared the field using wooden ploughs that were pulled by oxen. The plough turned the soil to make it ready for planting. Farmers **sowed** the seeds for their plants and crops after the fields had been flooded by water from the rivers. This was because the water made the soil very **rich**. They were very skilled farmers and planted different crops in winter and summer.

Farmers kept **domesticated** animals such as sheep, goats, chickens, pigs, and maybe even donkeys and camels. They kept these animals for their meat, although they mostly ate fruit and vegetables.

HUNTING AND FISHING

Archaeologists know a lot about what Indus people ate from studying the bones and teeth of skeletons. They have discovered that, as well as eating fruit,

vegetables, and crops like wheat and barley, the Indus people also hunted animals for meat. They caught large animals like elephants and rhinos in big traps and hunted other animals using spears, slingshots, and bows and arrows. The meat was probably cooked over a fire in the village or city and eaten with other food such as lentils.

BY STUDYING THE TEETH FROM SKELETONS, HISTORIANS KNOW THAT MEN IN THE INDUS VALLEY ATE MORE THAN WOMEN.

HUNTERS IN THE INDUS VALLEY HAD TO BE VERY CAREFUL. THERE WERE MANY **PREDATORS** IN THE WILD, INCLUDING SNAKES, CROCODILES, AND TIGERS.

Some people worked along the coast or riverbanks and hunted ducks and other wild birds that lived near the water. Fishermen used nets to catch fish, such as carp. Archaeologists have found many seafood shells amongst the animal bones and plant seeds, which suggest that fishermen also collected and ate shellfish.

ARTS AND CRAFTS

JEWELRY

SOME people in the Indus Valley worked as craft workers. Children usually had the same job as their parents, who taught them the craft while the children were still young. They made sculptures, clothing, pots, fishing nets, and jewelry. Jewelry was very popular, and people wore necklaces, earrings, bracelets and **amulets**. They made their jewelry from gold, silver, precious stones, shells, and a type of rock called soapstone. Bracelets made from conch shells were very popular and are still made in India.

BRACELET

POTTERY

Pots, bowls, and cups were very useful in everyday life in the Indus Valley. People used them to eat from and to store food in. They were usually made from clay and were shaped on a potter's wheel before being baked in a hot oven to harden. Most pots were left plain, but some were colored yellow, green, blue, or red and were decorated with patterns of leaves or flowers. Pottery and jewelry were often taken by Indus Valley traders to different lands to be exchanged with other traders.

SCULPTURE

There were no temples or **tombs** built by the Indus people, but they did make many small sculptures of gods, kings, people, and animals. They were made from metal and clay and may have been used in religious ceremonies or for children to play with.

There are now only a few Indus sculptures left, and one of these is the "priest king" sculpture. The "priest king" was found in a small house in Mohenjo-daro in 1927. The statue is only about 7 inches (17.5 cm) tall and is carved from stone. Historians think that it may represent an Indus ruler, but no one knows for certain.

The Ochre Colored Pottery culture (OCP) was a period that occurred towards the end of the Indus Valley Civilization, during the Late Harappan era. Some historians believe that OCP culture was part of the culture of the Indus Valley Civilization, while others see it as a culture of its own.

THE OCHRE COLORED POTTERY CULTURE INCLUDED SOME SCULPTURES MADE FROM BRONZE, COPPER, AND *TERRACOTTA*.

WRITING

INDUS SCRIPT ON A UNICORN SEAL

People in the Indus Valley wrote by scratching characters and symbols into soft clay using a pointed stick or sharp tool. They used around 400 different pictures to represent different things. Their writing system was called the Indus script and it is the oldest form of writing ever to be found in India and Pakistan. Historians believe that only a few people, called scribes, knew how to read and write but they may have taught other people in small schools. Not a lot of writing has been found from the Indus Valley Civilization – there were no books, stories, or laws – but it is thought that most writing was used to record things to do with trade, government, or religion. For example, goods exchanged by traders had different seals on them, which historians believe said what each product was and who was buying it.

TRADERS COULD READ ENOUGH TO KNOW WHAT WAS WRITTEN ON THE SEALS OF DIFFERENT GOODS.

Indus script has been found on seals, pottery, and even bones, but people still do not know what language the Indus people spoke and wrote in. Historians have not been able to read or ***translate*** any Indus script to work out what it says, so much of the Indus Valley Civilization is still a mystery.

In 1799, a large stone was found by French soldiers in Egypt. The stone had the same text carved into it written in three different languages: Greek, Egyptian *hieroglyphics*, and Demotic, a type of Egyptian writing. Up until this point, historians had not been able to read hieroglyphic writing, but in the 1820s, a man called Jean François-Champollion was able to read the hieroglyphs by using the Greek text. People could now read and understand other texts written in hieroglyphics and learn more about ancient Egypt.

THIS STONE IS KNOWN AS THE ROSETTA STONE.

THE END OF THE INDUS VALLEY

SOME AREAS OF PRESENT-DAY INDIA HAVE VERY BAD FLOODING.

THE Indus Valley Civilization was at its strongest between 2600 and 1900 B.C., but shortly after this, between 1900 and 1700 B.C., the civilization came to an end. Historians are not sure exactly how or why this happened, but they think many different factors may have contributed to it.

ARCHAEOLOGISTS HAVE STUDIED SKELETONS AND FOUND THAT MANY PEOPLE IN THE INDUS VALLEY DIED FROM MALARIA, A DISEASE THAT IS SPREAD BY MOSQUITOES.

Some historians believe that natural disasters led to the end of the Indus Valley. A change to the Indus River's path may have caused either flooding or drought in the region, which would have affected farming. Crops would have failed and the Indus people would have starved as there would have been nothing to eat. The flooding would have also disrupted the cities' plumbing and sewage systems. This may have caused waste to rise up into the streets, leading to the quick spread of disease.

By around 1500 B.C., the Indus cities had been abandoned. Many farmers were still living in the small villages in the countryside, but the cities had become impossible to live in. They quickly became very overcrowded and there was not enough space for all the people living there. New houses were built on top of old houses and important buildings, like the Great Bath in Mohenjo-daro. It was difficult to keep up with so many new houses, and many stopped getting repaired. Drains blocked up and were no longer emptied, so the cities became very dirty and smelly. Eventually, wind, rain, and flooding washed away many of the mud bricks until just a few remained.

INDUS VALLEY RUINS

The abandonment of the cities may partly have been due to the Indus Valley Civilization stopping trading with Mesopotamia. There would have been less work for people like traders and merchants, which might have made the cities poorer and caused people to move away.

THE LEGACY OF THE INDUS VALLEY

ALTHOUGH the Indus Valley Civilization came to an end around 3,500 years ago, and little is known about the people and the society, it has still contributed a lot to the modern world. One of these contributions is how the Indus religion influenced some parts of modern Hinduism. Historians know that the Indus people worshipped a "mother goddess" who some people believe is similar to the Hindu mother goddess, sometimes called Parvati. The Indus people prayed to their mother goddess and believed that she gave health and *fertility* to people, plants, and animals.

The Indus people believed that the cow was a special animal because it gave them meat and milk. Cows were very important in the Indus religion and the people saw them as givers of life because of the food they could get from them. Hindus today view cows as being sacred animals and are taught that they should not harm or eat cows.

ZEBU CATTLE IN INDIA ARE A BREED OF COW THAT WAS COMMON IN THE INDUS VALLEY THOUSANDS OF YEARS AGO. THEY ARE STILL IMPORTANT IN HINDUISM TODAY.

COTTON

Clothes, towels, and bedsheets can all be made from cotton, a type of plant that grows in India, Africa, and the Americas. People in the Indus Valley were the first in the world to *cultivate* cotton plants and begin growing them to be used to make cloth. Farmers in the countryside grew cotton in the fields and craft workers in the city wove the cotton into clothing and other products. These could be used by Indus people or taken to other cities and civilizations by traders where they could be exchanged.

Some cotton threads found in India and Pakistan are believed to be over 5,000 years old and the method of spinning cotton into thread did not change much for many years. Today, cotton is used all over the world and is a useful material for making most of the clothes we wear.

COTTON FIELD

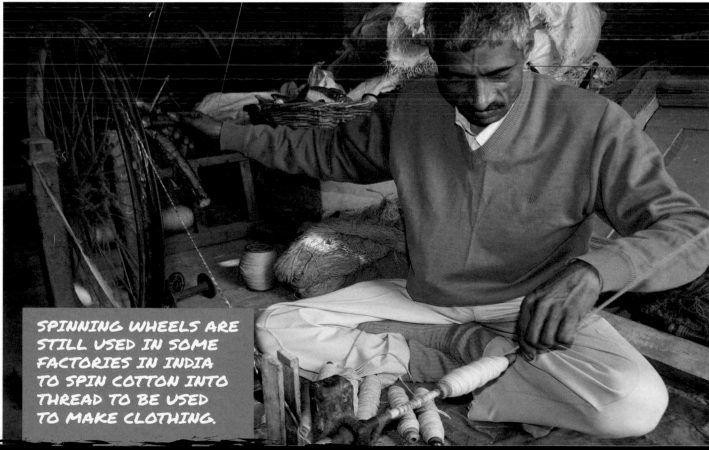

SPINNING WHEELS ARE STILL USED IN SOME FACTORIES IN INDIA TO SPIN COTTON INTO THREAD TO BE USED TO MAKE CLOTHING.

TIMELINE OF THE

4000 B.C.

PEOPLE BEGIN FARMING IN THE INDUS VALLEY

3800-1500 B.C.

FARMERS SETTLE IN HARAPPA

3000 B.C.

GROUPS OF PEOPLE DEVELOP THE FIRST VILLAGES IN THE INDUS VALLEY

1900-1700 B.C.

THE INDUS VALLEY CIVILIZATION BEGINS TO FALL APART

1900-1300 B.C.

LATE HARAPPAN ERA

1500 B.C.

ALL INDUS VALLEY CITIES ARE ABANDONED BY THIS POINT

INDUS VALLEY

3000-2000 B.C.

THE GREAT BATH IS BUILT IN MOHENJO-DARO DURING THE 3RD MILLENNIUM B.C.

2600 B.C.

THE INDUS VALLEY CIVILIZATION BEGINS AROUND THIS TIME

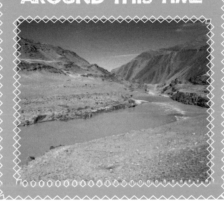

2500 B.C.

THE INDUS VALLEY CIVILIZATION REACHES ITS HEIGHT

A.D. 1826

HARAPPA IS FIRST REDISCOVERED

A.D. 1922

MOHENJO-DARO IS FIRST REDISCOVERED

A.D. 1927

THE "PRIEST KING" SCULPTURE IS FOUND IN MOHENJO-DARO

MAP OF THE INDUS VALLEY

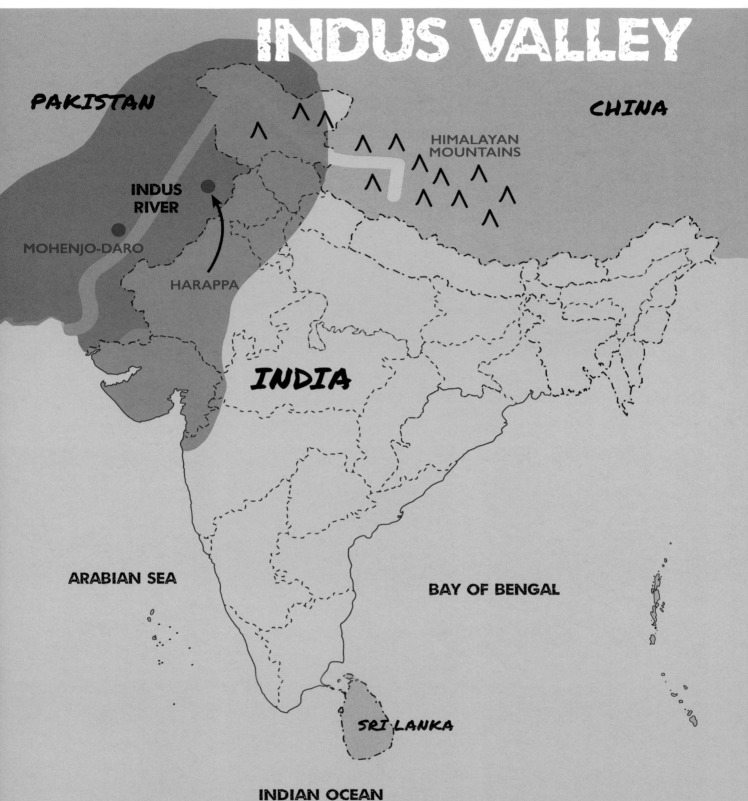

PAKISTAN

CHINA

INDUS
RIVER

HIMALAYAN
MOUNTAINS

MOHENJO-DARO

HARAPPA

INDIA

ARABIAN SEA

BAY OF BENGAL

SRI LANKA

INDIAN OCEAN

INDUS VALLEY

GLOSSARY

A.D.	"in the year of the lord", marks the time after Christians believe Jesus was born
amulets	pieces of jewelry thought to protect the against evil, danger, or disease
archaeologists	historians who study buried ruins and ancient objects in order to learn about human history
B.C.	meaning "before Christ", it is used to mark dates that occurred before Christians believe Jesus was born
breed	a group of animals in the same species that have similar characteristics
cattle	cows and bulls
citadel	a strong building, like a castle, built on a high place near a city
civilizations	the societies, cultures, and ways of life of certain areas
climate	the common weather conditions in certain places
cultivate	grow and care for a plant or crop
domesticated	referring to animals that are tamed so that they can be kept by humans
drought	a long period of very little rainfall, which leads to a lack of water
expensive	costing a lot of money
famines	when large numbers of people do not have enough food
fertile	soil where plants and crops can easily be grown
fertility	the ability to have children
government	the group of people with the authority to run a country and decide its laws
grid system	laid out in a grid, with straight lines that cross each other at 90 degrees
hieroglyphics	a type of writing used by the ancient Egyptians that used symbols and images
kiln	an oven that is used for hardening, burning, or drying something
loincloths	strips of cloth worn around the loins and hips
peasants	poor land workers who belonged to the lowest social class
predators	animals that hunt other animals for food
purity	to be pure and free from any imperfections or defects
reservoirs	a large natural or man-made lake used as a source of water supply
rich	having a lot of material wealth
sacred	connected to a god or gods
seals	designs that are stamped onto soft material, like wax
settlements	places people live permanently, like villages or towns
sowed	planted in the ground
stories	levels of a building
taxes	payments made to the government so that they can provide services
terracotta	a hard, brown-red type of clay used to make pottery, bricks, and sculptures
tombs	places for the burial of the dead
translate	change the words of one language into another language to understand it
wealthy	having lots of money

INDEX